Once, there was a canal.

Once, there was a canal.

by Liza Hyatt

Chatter House Press
Indianapolis, Indiana

Once, there was a canal.

Copyright© 2017 by Liza Hyatt

Cover design by Gary Schmitt, Schmitt Design, Inc.
shmittdesign@ymail.com

Cover art by Wilson Reed Berry (1851-1928), Wabash and Erie Canal at E. Market Street, Logansport, IN. Provided courtesy of the Cass County Historical Society.

All rights reserved.

Except for brief quotations embodied in critical articles and reviews in newspapers, magazines, radio or television, no part of this book may be reproduced in any form or by any means electronic, mechanical, or by any information storage and retrieval system without written permission from the publisher.

For information:

Chatter House Press
7915 S Emerson Ave, Ste B303
Indianapolis, IN 46237

chatterhousepress.com

ISBN: 978-1-937793-44-9
Library of Congress Control Number: 2017950862

For Margaret Heffernan Hyatt,
grandmother we called Bokey,
who wrote poetry
and preserved the stories
of her Irish grandparents.

And for her son,
Paul Winton Hyatt,
my father,
with whom I share
a love of history,
and of walking
both often-used
and newly discovered
paths.

Acknowledgments:

The researching and writing of these poems was made possible, in part, with support from the Indiana Arts Commission and the National Endowment for the Arts, a federal agency.

The author presented these poems in bardic style with harp accompaniment in March 2016 at the Wabash County History Museum, Wabash Indiana and in April 2016 at the annual meeting of the Wabash and Erie Canal Center in Delphi, Indiana. The Indiana Arts Commission approved these presentations as official Bicentennial Legacy projects.

I give heartfelt thanks to my new-found 4th cousin Marge Graham for her help with Meehan genealogy; to Bob and Carolyn Schmidt for all that they have compiled for the Canal Society of Indiana; to Dan McCain and Terry Lacy of the Wabash and Erie Canal Center in Delphi Indiana; and Tom Castaldi, Allen County Historian who knows the northern half of the canal better than the back of his hand. The interviews they provided were of immeasurable help. Without their assistance, this project would have quickly become a boat in low water, stuck in the mud, going nowhere.

Thanks also to Cass County Historical Society for permission to use the painting by Wilson Reed Berry (1851-1928) depicting the Wabash and Erie Canal and E. Market Street in Logansport, IN.

Commendations

Liza Hyatt reflected on her Irish ancestors' journey to the U.S. and work on the Indiana canal, read long on the subject, stood where they toiled, and wrote poems telling their story, her story, a part of our story. To witness the ongoing journey of her voice(s) in the telling of this ancestral tale in these new epic poems that reach mythic timelessness is a marvel. Once, There Was a Canal is a breakthrough for Liza Hyatt, a gift to us and our descendants.

— Norbert Krapf, former Indiana Poet Laureate

"I follow towpath and canal bed remnants, the old portage, / the glacial plain, all the way to the lichened-limestone old lock / at Lagro," Liza Hyatt writes in Once, There Was a Canal, a poetry book that is essentially a pilgrimage to find and understand the story of the poet's great-great grandparents—Irish immigrants to Indiana who helped build the Wabash and Erie Canal. As the poet marshals history, quotation, myth, and, most of all, the power of her own vivid imagination to tell Daniel and Kate's story, we become aware that the past is embedded in the present. The hopes, fears and labors of these 19th century immigrants connect us more deeply to the Indiana landscape and to the struggles of displaced people in our own time.

— Shari Wagner, Indiana Poet Laureate, 2016-2017

A Brief Note from the Author

In these poems, I endeavor to be as historically accurate as possible while imagining the story of my paternal great-great grandparent's lives. I began with only a short family narrative, written by my grandmother about her father's parents, Daniel Heffernan and Catherine Meehan. We have no photographs of them. No letters were saved. To enter their story, many missing details had to be imagined and inferred. The art of poetry writing helped me do this re-imagining. I have found words for what Daniel and Catherine and other family members might have said to tell their story to me. I have invented what they might have read and written in letters I know them to have received and sent. In doing so, I have come much closer to knowing the truth about the struggles they endured, the losses they experienced, the strength they found to overcome hardship and prosper.

At the end of this book, I include an afterword that gives a complete description of my writing process, choices I made, and how I translated historical research into poetry. Whenever I read works of historical fiction, I want to know what the author invented and what was based on historical records. I wrote this book's afterword with such curious readers in mind. I also provide some brief endnotes about specific poems that rely heavily upon language found within historical documents. And for the most avid canal history buffs, I have compiled a bibliography listing resources that were essential to my understanding of the 19th century and the building of the Wabash and Erie Canal.

CONTENTS

Part One - Surveying

Poet's Prayer 3
From Niamh of the Golden Hair 4
Provisions for My Poet's Journey 7
I Call Across Time to Daniel Heffernan 9
Daniel Heffernan Calls to Me 11
The Path of the Earliest Surveyor, 1765 13
From A Letter to His Excellency George Washington 15
What the Governors Said – Hendricks, Ray, Noble, 1822-34 17
What Governors Never Say 18
Upon News of the Passage of the General Internal Improvement Bill - 1836 19

Part Two - Voyages on the Ancestral Path

First Morning of a Writing Retreat 23
Following the Ancestral Path 25
Anne Heffernan Says Goodbye to Her Brother, 1837 28
Daniel's Boat Floats Free From Its Moorings 30
Immram Catherine Meehann (The Voyage of Catherine Meehan) 32
Great-Great-Great Grandmother Ellen Leonard Meehan *34*

Part Three - From Summit City to Star City

Summit City Pilgrimage 39
Heading West On US 24, at the Allen-Whitley County Line 41
While Sitting on the Old Lock at Lagro 42
Near Cicott's Mill, September 1838 43
Immram of the Nineteenth Century 45
Daniel Joins the Whigs at Tippecanoe Battlefield , May 1840 46
Packet Boat Travel: Two Perspectives 48
How We Met – Kate's Version 50
How Daniel Courted Kate, 1843 52
Catherine Meehan Heffernan Described in a Few Words 53
Kate's Story While Shopping at Purdue, Brown, and Co. 54
Daniel at the Canal Dock 56
Our History Keepers 57

Part Four - Our Misfortune Rather Than Fault

How Others Described the Irish 61
The Great Hunger – An Gorta Mór 63
Letter from Tipperary, Winter 1846 64
Newly Married Kate Takes Matters in Her Own Hands, 1847 66
Michael Heffernan Fills in Some Missing Details, 1848 67
Kate's Middle of the Night Confession 69
Cholera, August 1849 71

Part Five - In Pike and Daviess County

What Daniel Read and Responded To 75
Daniel Describes His Work, 1851 77
Letter from Kate to John Purdue, Summer 1852 79
John Purdue's Response 81
Daniel, Summer Dusk on the Homestead 82
Nearing Sixty, Kate Speaks of Her Children 84
When I Ask for More of Her Story 87
Two-Thousand Grandmothers 89
What My Great-Great Grandparents Touched 90
At Ninety-Two, Daniel Looks Back 92
Communion 94

Appendices

Afterword: A Poet's Pilgrimage on the Wabash and Erie Canal 99
Notes 105
Canal Era Bibliography and Resources 107
Wabash and Erie Canal: 1832 – 1876 109
About the Author 111
Previous Publications 113

Once, there was a canal.

PART ONE

SURVEYING

It is not down on any map; true places never are.

--Herman Melville

Not I, not anyone else can travel that road for you,
You must travel it for yourself.
It is not far, it is within reach,
Perhaps you have been on it since you were born and did not know.
Perhaps it is everywhere on water and on land.

--Walt Whitman

Part One - Surveying

Once, there was a canal.

Poet's Prayer

May my imagination
be a seaworthy vessel
that brings me,
an immigrant
with passport
writ in blood and bone,
into a current strong
with ancestral voices,
and onto the shores
of deep listening.

From Niamh of the Golden Hair*

From Tír na nÓg I feel your questioning.
You draw near to where the space between worlds is thin
and time moves in whorls and spiral rings.

You need to know where people go when they die.
You need to know if you will remember yourself,
if you will remember anything,
if you will be alone, or nothing,
or aware of everything when you die.

You ask how long you have to live.
You ask how deep roots go
and if what you have chosen
furthers what your grandmothers
and great grandmothers loved,
what they birthed and suffered
but could not complete.

You ask how deep roots go
and if your life honors your grandfather's
and great grandfather's toil and search for justice.

You need to feel how the past nests inside the present,
how the future already exists inside the past.
You long to dance with the spirit world all around you
as you breathe air crowded with ancestral ghosts.

You walk a trail where once a canal
was built by these ghosts.
You almost hear them calling to each other,
the scrape of shovels against root and rock.
You almost taste the dirt and sweat
on their arms, their bearded cheeks.

Once, there was a canal.

You need them to pause from their digging
and feel you here with them. You need them
to see you, to see people hurrying past
in cities full with their descendants,
then turn again to the hard work of digging,
dreaming of you as you dream of them.

I have brought you here
to show you how all times are co-occurring,
how all places contain doorways connecting worlds.
I will teach you how each footstep
touches the brown fields of Indiana
and the green hills of Ireland,
the deep woods of the First People,
the great waves of the deep sea,
the shadow glades of Tír na nÓg.

You will need the wild horse of imagination,
as briny and restless as sea froth,
as sinewed as instinct.

Hold fast to imagination with your body,
hands entwined in its mane, and you will journey
as far into myth and mystery as any hero might.

But once you begin, your life is bound to imagination.
I warn you: Should you try to forget,
let go of the wild beast to sleep a dreamless sleep
and stand again on solid, linear soil,
then everything will cease moving,
your skin wither, your dry bones turn to dust.

You must travel forever, beyond life, beyond death,
or not at all and once you begin, not even
the silver apples of the moon,
the golden apples of the sun
will quench your longing.

Part One - Surveying

But I see you have already chosen,
taken the white mane in your hands.
You are pulling yourself up to the quivering back,
wrapping your arms around imagination's dappled neck,
legs around imagination's fierce belly.

Let the wild journey begin.

* In Irish mythology, Niamh is the daughter of Manannan mac Lir and one of the queens of Tír na nÓg, the Land of Youth. She crossed the Western Sea on a magic horse, Embarr, (whose name means imagination) and asked famed Irish harper-poet-warrior Oisín to return to Tír na nÓg with her. He lived with her for several years, and when he returned to Ireland, he found hundreds of years had passed in Ireland.

Provisions for My Poet's Journey

A three-page story
of Irish immigrants,
gathered and typed
by my grandmother
about her paternal grandparents,
Daniel and Kate Heffernan,
pioneers who helped make
the longest canal ever built
in North America.

A need to connect to people
through deep conversation,
which made me a therapist
listening to suffering,
learning how to grieve,
the deepest way to listen.

A desire to know –
after much loss –
the foundation on which I stand,
the worldview seen
from the shoulders of ancestors.

A question, seeded in childhood:
How and why is it that history,
memory, and imagination overlap?

Part One - Surveying

A desire to time-travel
to America in the nineteenth century.
My delight that I now have a story
that describes my family in that time,
a story I am called to visit
and bring to life.

A longing to walk old ways as pilgrim,
to encounter grace in chance moments,
enter wholly unexpected places
and find them holy.

I Call Across Time to Daniel Heffernan

I'm told you were a good storyteller,
but only one in your own words,
from your farming days,
was written down and passed on.

Late at night, with your neighbor Griffin,
in a wagon pulling its load
over rough and muddy roads,
you were both singing
loudly, drunk and out of tune,
as you bounced along.

Griffin offered to help with the horses
while he sobered up a bit
before walking home across the fields,
and you responded,
"No, I'll do it, so I'll smell more of horse
and not so much of liquor.
If Kate smells me the way I am,
she'll raise cane all night."

And so Griffin set off
and you curried down the horses,
then went to the well for a drink of water,
but in the distance you heard a commotion
and Griffin calling "Suey, suey!"

Part One - Surveying

You staggered downhill
and found him floundering
on the ground in his pigpen,
the pigs feasting on what spilled
from his now empty jug of whiskey.
And Griffin, as you helped him to his feet,
said to the pigs, "To be sure, it is good, but begors,
you'll have an awful headache in the morning."

You must have repeated this story for Kate, your children,
your grandchildren, laughing and making fun of yourself
so many times that this story was told at your funeral.

We hold onto this scrap of humor.
But this can't be all you hoped we'd remember.
And so I am calling to you,
down the hill, down the field of time:
What else made you laugh? What songs did you sing?
What are your stories of struggle and salvation,
love and grief? Come to my call;
lift the past back onto its feet.
Help me reclaim your life story for my inheritance.

Once, there was a canal.

Daniel Heffernan Calls to Me

You carry scraps of stories,
and longing to know more,
you dare to ask the dead to speak.

We seem unreachable,
whispering only,
without clear voices,
from a remote place.

We are touched, great-great granddaughter,
that though your elders did not know
to teach you how to find us,
you've begun to wander
in search of the invisible
channels and bridges
we ancestors build through time.

Listen, Liza, and look.
We are always close.
We need to breathe
our stories into you,
but you must make
your whole self ready
to live in a world
full of singing spirits.

You must learn all
you can about our
hungers and poverty,
our sea roads and towpaths,
our miasmas and diaspora,

Part One - Surveying

        and come to see your laughter
        and tears rippling out
        from our struggles.

        Now, in the middle of life,
        guided only by our whispers,
        help us repair the old bridges,
        reconnect our shores, clear
        tangled overgrowth, dredge
        debris, and dig the canals
        through which our stories will finally flow.

Once, there was a canal.

The Path of the Earliest Surveyor, 1765

There were no roads.
Rivers were the easier way to go
when they were deep from the flow
of fresh rain in spring and fall.

For a few weeks every year, our canoes could carry
pelts and guns, beads and knives
over high fast water
without rapids and riffs to tangle with.

There was the portage at the carrying place
between the Miami and the Ouabache.
Plentiful rains made these rivers swell
over this higher land
and we carried canoes and goods
on our backs for only a few miles.

There were rattlesnakes five feet long
and bee trees pocketed with golden combs.
Men died of malaria and snake venom here.
We could kill the old snakes
but the mosquitoes were sure to bite

and still, it was here,
that I, a man with honey on his lips
was lulled to sleep by muttering thunder
and rain pattering on tent canvas.

Part One - Surveying

> It was here, among wild hemp
> and the white flash of sycamore in blue sky and sun,
> fog lifting through the trees like wool being carded,
>
> that I woke,
> and declared myself to be
> in some of the world's finest country,
> licking into each word
> a wild, lingering sweetness.

Once, there was a canal.

From A Letter to His Excellency George Washington

London, February 5, 1797

Sir, looking forward to that period
when the whole force of your Mind
will Act upon the Internal improvement of our Country,
by Promoting Agriculture and Manufactures:
I have little doubt but easy Conveyance,
the Great agent to other improvements,
will have its due weight And meet your patronage.

For the mode of giving easy Communication
to every part of the American States
I draw your attention to Creative Canals.
The expanded mind will trace down the time
when they will penetrate every district,

Bringing Water Carriage within the easy Reach
of every house, nor would any house
be more than 10 or 14 miles from a Canal,
each State commencing a Creative System,
filling the whole Country,
in Less than a Century bringing
Water Carriage within easy Cartage
of every Acre of the American States,
conveying the Surplus Labours of
one hundred Millions of Men,

Part One - Surveying

penetrating the Interior Country,
And binding the Whole
In the bonds of Social Intercourse.

The Importance of this Subject will plead
my excuse of troubling you with So long a Letter,
And in expectation of being Favoured
with your thoughts on the System,

I remain with the utmost Esteem and Sincere Respect,
Your most obedient Servant

Robt. Fulton

What the Governors Said – Hendricks, Ray, Noble, 1822-34

Frontier travel was burdensome,
dangerous, life-threatening
so Hendricks urged us:
to "not lose sight of those great objects,
the navigation of the falls of the Ohio,
the improvement of the Wabash,
the White rivers, and other streams,
and the construction of
the national and other roads"
that would bring settlers to the land.

Ray insisted:
that "the rough appearances of nature
must be overcome
and made to yield
to human enterprise.
Our waters must be imprisoned
in new channels,
and made to subserve
the essential purposes of commerce."

And Noble reasoned:
that since New York, Pennsylvania and Ohio
were building canals
"with little more means or resources
than their public credit"
and were being "repaid many fold"
by "increased demands and higher prices"
for corn, wheat, timber, hides, shingles, whiskey,
we too should borrow, throw money
into "circulation in payment for labor, materials, and subsistence"
and begin immediately to make people richer
because the wealth "of a well-managed government"
is not found in "sums hoarded in the Treasury"
but in "the pockets of the people."

Part One - Surveying

What Governors Never Say

We have no idea what it will cost.

It is a feat of engineering
that must be worked out
as it is built.

Those who say it is
a foolish venture
are probably right
but this is the best
we can come up with.

We are underestimating
the cost of building it
and have scarcely considered
the cost of maintaining it.

Once again we are
rushing into things with
our usual mix of
bold ingenuity,
fantasy, greed,
zealous faith, and
blind hubris.

And nature refuses to be subservient,
has never yet been fully overcome,
and droughts, ice,
spring thaws, storms, floods,
and burrowing animals
will ground our boats,
collapse towpaths and berms,
destroy dams,
bankrupt us, and break
imprisoned nature free.

Once, there was a canal.

Upon News of the Passage
of the General Internal Improvement Bill - 1836

All across the state,
in Washington, Indianapolis,
Connersville, Logansport, Peru,
we banqueted, orated,
set off cannons, built bonfires,
paraded up and down
cold winter streets,
bands playing,
our courthouses lit
from cellar to garret.

In Evansville,
we unfurled a long pennant
with the words
Internal Improvements
stitched by ladies who
sewed feverishly day and night
to see it raised by an official committee,
our cheers resounding,
guns roaring,
processions forming.

In towns projected to be
on the line of the canals,
we bubbled and effervesced,
we reveled all night long
joy beaming on our countenances,
generous, unanimous, gushing joy,
with which, in toast after
barrel-draining toast,
we proclaimed
the state of Indiana to be
like Pallas from the brain of Jove,
springing into existence,
full grown and vigorous,
destined to be one of the brightest stars

Part One - Surveying

    in the firmament of
    our widely extended
    and happy Republic.

    From every house, hamlet, and shanty
    our joy was made manifest
    by the simultaneous glow of light,
    candles and lanterns burning
    from humble windows,
    presenting the most beautiful illumination
    we ever witnessed.

    All along the Wabash,
    from newly built cabins, farms,
    and only just platted towns,
    where, but twelve months ago,
    little else was to be seen
    save dense wilderness,
    we sent forth vivid streams of light
    our hearts brimming
    with cherished and lively hopes
    for civilization's cheer
    and our own future prosperity.

PART TWO

VOYAGES ON THE ANCESTRAL PATH

May the nourishment of the earth be yours,
May the clarity of light be yours,
May the fluency of the ocean be yours,
May the protection of the ancestors be yours.

--John O' Donohue

It may be that when we no longer know what to do
we have come to our real work,

and that when we no longer know which way to go
we have come to our real journey.

--Wendell Berry

Part Two - Voyages on the Ancestral Path

Once, there was a canal.

First Morning of a Writing Retreat

I have rented a straw bale cabin
to write a winter communion
with ancestors and the old gods of Earth.

On the wall, someone has hung
a watercolor of an old stone bridge
and I see Burnett's Creek arch,
or the culvert over Prairie Creek.

On another wall:
a painting of two boats
docked near a wood-frame house,
packet boats near the lock-keeper's quarters.

The window here looks out
at shapes like standing stones,
the old abutments of an abandoned bridge,
as if Daniel and time have been here
working and unworking.

Such gifts spark my imagination,
seem given by the muse.
As the sunrise flames over the lake
I start the day by reading about Brighid,
Celtic goddess of poetry, healing,
and all things forged in sacred fire.

I wonder if her name and the word bridge
are cousins sharing the same root
and learn that Brighid is goddess
of all things elevated, hills and hill forts,
and ever-rising fire.

Part Two - Voyages on the Ancestral Path

I pronounce the words
in the old way: Breed and breeg,
and hear water flowing from a spring
and footsteps on wooden planks
crossing a stream to reach its sacred source.

All year names like Canal Street
and Towpath Road in inland cities
named as ports, have led me to
traces of old ways, canal prism remnants
beside modern roads, the stonework
of a long-gone aqueduct supporting
a still-used train trestle.

I long for this pilgrimage to carry me
back to the old lands where places are named
Bridport and Bridewell Lane
and Little Bredy, and Long Bredy,
and nearby paths lead to chapels built near springs
where women kept and still keep
the fires burning.

For now I watch the sun
turn lake ice to smelted iron
and pray the day's writing
will be blessed, the ancient muse
bridging my world to hers.

Following the Ancestral Path

1.

The eyes travel the path
across the page,
reading stories,
reading maps,
learning, getting lost in
the topography of time,
tracking milestones
and landmarks of the past,
discovering a disintegrating
trail of crumbs, traces
of those who left home
and wandered out of sight,
out of memory.

2.

The mind travels the path,
unraveling threads,
intersections,
choices and turns,
speeding down wide avenues,
halted by dead-ends,
circling back around,
mindscapes, dark caves, deserts,
where tracks are lost,
valleys ready for harvest,
crowded cities, street grids,
finding, losing the way,
searching, and researching
history's remnants,
our scars, some healing.

Part Two - Voyages on the Ancestral Path

3.

The hand travels the path,
pen over paper, writing notes,
charting, recharting,
mind forays, thought trails,
piecing together
memorizing, mapping,
excavating lost tales,
cartographer of old world and new,
words of where and when,
change and struggle,
scribblings,
transparencies of wind,
bone runes,
ink of blood and eons.

4.

With pilgrim soles,
feet travel the path,
knapsack of dense rye bread,
apples, sour cheese,
sun, rain and icy gusts,
the tattered coat,
the walking stick,
the broken-in boots,
wanderer of far and fair lanes,
strider of roads, hills, burrens,
chalk trails, towpaths,
cobblestones, asphalt,
retracing past paths,
old ways, giving
fealty to other feet
that wore grass and rock away,
a rushing stream
of sandals, moccasins, and boots
carving channels in earth
as restlessly as wind and water.

5.

The imagination travels the path,
seer in the soul, sea-faring,
deep-diving, the soul
that calls and has always
called for every journey,
every path, every trek
through time, world and wonder,
two wings, living world,
underworld, always opening,
always closing, dying,
being born, night walker,
dark vision, descending.

6.

The breathing body travels the path,
walks, one foot in the world,
one foot in the dream,
one foot in the present,
one foot in the past,
one foot in wanderlust,
one foot in wonder lost,
one foot touching earth, soil, pavement, rock,
one foot touching shadow, soul, song-line, ghost.

Anne Heffernan Says Goodbye to Her Brother, 1837

We three were going to leave for America together.
But now we watch only Daniel
walk slowly down the lane.
Mother weeps; I reach for her hand;
and Michael calls to our brother,
"Don't forget your promise!"

A marriage proposal changed my fate;
I chose to stay in Tipperary,
Michael gave his passage money
for my dowry, and Daniel swore
to send his earnings
so that Michael can join him.

Our hearts are full of questions.
Will Daniel survive, struggle, prosper?
Has Michael lost his only chance to leave?
Will I regret this marriage, have children,
live to see them grow…?

Nearly two hundred years later,
you, one of our descendants,
are as unable as I am
to see beyond this moment.

You must imagine me here, forever parting,
as the past allots you only the questions
my future demands of me.

Once, there was a canal.

No other trace of me remains.

Search the archives.

Every voyage you make
seeking the green hills
and stone house
of my story
founders.

Daniel's Boat Floats Free From Its Moorings

Wind fills the sails' canvas lungs;
the current pulls the ship out and away;
the searoad is ancient, pulsing.

On board, on deck,
several beside me have covered
their faces to weep.

Eyes fixed on shore,
I watch diminish,
the land where we were born,

where, though we swore
we would travel together,
or not at all,
my brother and sister
have chosen to stay,

and here, now, alone
in a crowd of immigrants,
I watch all that was familiar
shrink and melt into the horizon,
like a lump of hard candy
at the back of the mouth

knowing that soon,
here, now, alone
I will turn and face
the restless churning, deep unknown,
salt-spray pilgrim-tears on cheeks
as I lean into
the source of storms,
the whale-sung abyss
where I may drown.

Once, there was a canal.

And since I must do both,
I look to the past, which is being lost, behind,
I look to the future, where I will struggle, ahead,
adrift between them.

For endless days at sea.
Each of us, alone, between them.

For endless nights at sea.
Afraid between them.

Long after landfall, still not home,
adrift, alone, afraid, alive
between these shores.

Immram Catherine Meehann
(The Voyage of Catherine Meehan)

I was seven when our family left Co. Cork
and for seven weeks and more we sailed
and on the first day we watched
the green hills of the West,
from the stories of heroes and magic we love,
fade like a dream into the growing horizon.
Then it was into another west
beyond imagination, no land in sight,
only the sky, sea and restless change.

Ma and Da told us stories as we sailed,
to comfort us, to comfort themselves,
to convince our hearts, bodies aching
with separation, that we were brave,
not banished. Stories about
a better life where, when we
worked as hard as we always had,
we might find more than not drowning
in poverty's punishment, the most
we would achieve back home.

They told us stories of other voyagers,
of St. Brendan who sailed to the Land of Youth,
of Bran mac Feabhail who sailed on and on
to lands unknown because he would turn to ash
if he set foot in Ireland again. On days
when the sea did not toss us wildly
like an angry god, we emerged
from the belly of the ship into the sun,
and they opened our only book

and taught me to read the words boat, sea,
storm, rain, days, nights, dove and leaf.
Most nights I would fall asleep
curled into my grieving mother's warmth,
spelling these words in my mind,

Once, there was a canal.

knowing we were to be adrift longer than Noah,
feeling my mother and father's shaken faith
in some god-given promise of a future
wrapped around me like an old blanket,

learning from them how to make hope
grow out of loss and fear, how to carry it with me
like a scrap of green in the beak
of a strong, winged heart,
how to trust in flowing currents and wind and time
and our voyage toward an unsettled land
where life would grow
out of the ashes of sorrow
and begin anew.

Great-Great-Great Grandmother Ellen Leonard Meehan
Describes the Journey from Ireland to Fort Wayne

Our long weeks at sea
were slow, crowded, and cruel.
In the second week, baby Ann
and then three-year old Patrick,
woke burning with fever.
I did all I could, sat with them
through the night, praying.
But they were taken from us.
I cannot bear it, how we had to give
their little bodies to the comfortless deep.

I thought we'd left everything behind
and then, so soon,
death made us leave
these young ones,
so precious to us.
I wished we'd never left;
only John, my love for our older children,
and the kindness of other passengers
made me arrive safe ashore.

At last we sailed up the St. Lawrence.
We disembarked in Canada,
took the soonest possible passage
across to Ogdensburg, New York.

We boarded for a few weeks,
struggling, as John says,
to learn the lay of the land,
to get our bearings, to find
for what, at such great cost,
Providence brought us to America.

Once, there was a canal.

It wasn't long before we met
an agent for the Wabash and Erie Canal
who offered to pay our transportation to Indiana,
in exchange for a lien on wages earned
if John, my husband, and John, my son,
agreed to work for the canal, at ten dollars a month.
More enticing than the prospect of work
was talk of ample acres of land,
to be opened for settlement
and made available to canal men
for purchase at favorable rates.

My heart was sore and heavy,
and I didn't know if I had it in me
to travel hundreds more miles,
but as we searched,
it was clear the young state of Indiana
does not have enough men
to meet the canal's need for labor
and her people might welcome
new immigrants to help settle the state.

Both my Johns convinced me we must go.
We sailed up the river to Quebec and Montreal,
then onto Lake Ontario and by canal to Buffalo
and across Lake Erie to Toledo,
and finally, to avoid being mired
in the mud of the Great Black Swamp,
we went by boat to Fort Wayne.

When we arrived in town, we heard talk
of sham agents who swindle new arrivals
out of their last dollars, and thanked God
we chanced to meet with honest men.

Part Two - Voyages on the Ancestral Path

    John and John are south of town,
    working, bunking in nearby camps.
    Eliza, Ellen, Mary, Kate and I
    are boarding in town,
    where more Irish, German,
    and eastern Americans arrive every day,
    joining the first settlers, Indians,
    and French traders.

    I did not expect to live on
    the frontier of our new country.
    Exhausted, sad, and homesick
    I do not know when, if ever,
    I will feel settled and light-hearted again.

PART THREE

FROM SUMMIT CITY TO STAR CITY

When I find a well-drawn character in fiction or biography
I generally take a warm personal interest in him, for the reason
that I have known him before – met him on the river.

   -- Mark Twain

The imagination cannot help but pursue a line in the land –
onwards in space, but also backwards in time to the histories
of a route and its previous followers…the land itself,
filled with letters, words, texts, songs, signs and stories…

   -- Robert MacFarlane

Part Three - From Summit City to Star City

Once, there was a canal.

Summit City Pilgrimage

I arrive where I need to be when I need to be there,
and someone ahead of me, searching for the same thing,
is here to help, welcoming me to the tribe of great-great
granddaughters, of canal builders, of the Irish diaspora.

The old fort stands unguarded. Inside, woodsmoke,
musket powder, sweat. The courtyard is thick
with French, English, Algonquian voices, memories
of Kekionga, garden of corn and squash, green and growing.

I stand where the aqueduct stood and feel myself swimming.
I follow towpath and canal bed remnants, the old portage,
the glacial plain, all the way to the lichened-limestone old lock
at Lagro. Irish diggers, German stone-cutters, packet boat travelers,
pass through, among them first Daniel, then Kate, on the way
to Logansport, Delphi, Lafayette, where they will first meet.

At Kin-com-a-ong, Paradise Spring, the treaty, the land,
being lost, being won, a young woman with shining dark hair,
sits under a tree, looks up from her cell phone with eyes that see
across centuries. Here is Tau-Cum-Wah greeting me, sister
of Little Turtle, mother of Chief Richardsville. Here also is another
great-great granddaughter, called by old ones, smiling in recognition
as the steam whistle grows louder, the world changing, black smoke
and glints of Pullman cars through trees, driving fast through the valley,
the whole town gathered where the tracks cross Main Street,
the Wabash Cannonball thundering through, coal cinders on skin, hair.

Part Three - From Summit City to Star City

Standing on a bridge over the rain-swollen river, I see time moving,
muddy with the run-off of clear-cut civilization, full of eddies and whorls,
under and over currents. I see time moving, in the fast approaching storm,
clouds circling, brewing, winds from the north, winds from the south
and east, wrapping round each other, the downpour so fast and heavy
I, the whole world, breathe underwater, swimming in time.

All the women I will ever meet are time. And all the men. And dreams.
As morning comes, I dream a man's Irish lilt, my great-great grandfather,
laughing "Well, hello there!" A braided stream, its currents crossing
and recrossing, the blond locks, red and tawny tresses
of all my grandmothers, plaited in with my own.

Once, there was a canal.

Heading West On US 24, at the Allen-Whitley County Line

To the south we see
gray chunks of limestone

squatting in ragged heaps
on flat and arid land.

Long before this road,
this quarry, the people

of White Raccoon's village
lived here until all

Miami were forced
from Indiana.

These piles of rock,
long-remembering

earth up-heaved,
sit unmoving, heavy,

the refusal to leave home
buried deep in the first

people's hearts, brought
to the surface as stone.

While Sitting on the Old Lock at Lagro

It took us centuries to become good
at moving canal boats up hill.

While we learned,
the impoverished and oppressed
fought over and over
against those with power.

Daniel and Kate left Ireland
and lived the rest of their
uphill battle lives working
their way down stream.

The canal they built
was soon abandoned.

To be kept strong enough
to handle immense pressure,
canal locks, like democracy,
require constant repair.

Even iron can buckle.

The forces that oppress
are outside and inside the gates.

Once, there was a canal.

Near Cicott's Mill, September 1838

All day as we dig
we watch pass by
hundreds of people,
some on horseback,
most on foot,
old ones, young ones,
Potawatomi,
kept from fleeing
back into forest shadows
by soldiers who force them
on this march.

Our shovel-loads feel heavier today.
Something more than swamp mud
and broken roots burdens us now.

We came here from Ireland
to work, earn our scrip,
and buy land with it,
enduring the dangers
of this ditch-digging
with hope our children
will live more freely
than we have for centuries.

Now we see children,
exhausted, shivering with fever,
limping, hundreds of miles
still to walk.

Part Three - From Summit City to Star City

They cannot stay
without hating the settlers
for stealing their lands,
without fighting to get it back.

They cannot leave
without being forced to,
broken hearted.

We could not stay,
could not leave,
but had to,
just the same.

Is there anywhere
a man displaced by conquest
can go to live without
displacing another man?

Once, there was a canal.

Immram of the Nineteenth Century

When we could no longer live
in the lands of our ancestors,
we sank into the hills,
melted into the forests,
walked trails of tears,
boarded haunted boats,
crowded coffin ships, starving,
slipping into fevered dreams,
nothing about our path clear,
marked, obvious, or manifest,
our obscure destinies
stumbled upon as hunger and oppression
forced us farther west, west, into the West.

Part Three - From Summit City to Star City

Daniel Joins the Whigs at Tippecanoe Battlefield, May 1840

In Ireland, it's a mere ten years
since Catholics could run for Parliament,
but most are too poor to have the vote.

I've been an American not quite three,
and here I am, in a crowd of men,
pushing a large, leather sphere
over trampled grass, shouting
"Keep the ball rolling!"

Campaign speeches are flowing
with promises to get us out
of the mess Old Hickory
and the Democrats have made.
I arrived in the Panic of '37,
and last year, another one.
I've found work,
but I'm never sure I'll be paid.

I won't be, if Van Buren wins,
but Harrison supports
internal improvements like the canal

and he's a frontiersman,
a hero, who like us,
has slogged through mud,
fought the wilderness,
built shelter, cleared land.

Once, there was a canal.

Like me, many a man here
will be casting his first vote
when election day comes.

For now the crowd is singing,
"…Van Buren may drink his champagne,
and have himself toasted, from Georgia to Maine"

and someone is prying open another barrel
and we push in and fill to the brim
our drinking gourds and tin cups
and we sing of log cabins,
hearts warm and true,
and I down the hard cider,
ladle up more, and join
toast after toast
for Old Tippecanoe.

Packet Boat Travel: Two Perspectives

1. Exhausted travelers write letters home

We are cramped and crowded. No privacy.
On the roof, we swelter, sitting on trunks, benches,
some dangling legs from the edge,
all ducking to avoid injury from low bridges.
Below, platters of simple food come round:
corn, turnips, greens,
pork chops cooked in grease,
bread and butter, pickles and coffee.
At night all the day's heat
settles down into a hot stuffy cabin,
our canvas berths stacked, in shelves, floor to ceiling,
a curtain drawn to make scant shelter for the ladies,
mosquitoes hatched in the mud puddles of Indiana
condensed into one humming ravenous swarm
all around everyone's hard, little beds.
Sleepless, we listen to the insect drone,
every cough, sneeze, snore, belch and fart,
in stagnant air, sweating as we never
ever dreamed a body could.

Once, there was a canal.

2. Looking back, 1920

We are the only ones left to tell our story.
Children then, we are nostalgic old ones now.
The boat becomes our Aladdin's lamp,
our lace-curtained, velvet-cushioned,
plush-carpeted, floating fairy palace:
chandeliers of sparkling glass,
woodwork of white filigree and gold gilding.
The cabin is transformed by the steward,
chambermaid and cabin boys
from sitting to dining to sleeping room,
meals served like those at a first class hotel,
table linens, fine china, silverware.
We are congenial passengers lounging on deck,
waving handkerchiefs at passing boats,
enjoying bird song, trees, flowers,
fields of grain, hills and valleys,
prosperous towns, warehouses full
of cloth, wool, paper, pearl pot ash.
Our packet glides along smooth waters,
gently sailing, bugles sounding, mules pulling
and we feel only the leisured pace of long ago,
not how, even then, that time rushed to oblivion.

How We Met – Kate's Version

You know a few dates and locations.
The Carrolton Bridge,
where Daniel worked,
was nearing completion in 1843,
when I travelled from Fort Wayne to Lafayette.
Two years later, we were married
by Rev. Michael J. Clark,
in Lafayette's newly mortared
St. Mary and Martha's Church.

You want to know how chance encounters
changed to courtship, how two strangers
became bride and groom
in a little church built by pioneers.

You imagine me travelling for days
on a crowded canal boat,
emerging for fresh air when we reach
the town of Carrolton on Wabash,
my brother John with me,
a canal man in search of work.

Daniel may have been there
bent over drawings and figures
in Mentzer's Tavern,
a foreman discussing his crew's progress
with contractor Reed Case.

You want our eyes to meet and spark,
my tired face, my laugh, my smile
to imprint Daniel's memory
so that weeks, months later,
when John is hired on a crew Daniel oversees,
he is delighted to find John's little sister
is the girl from the tavern
with the charming laugh, the flashing eyes.

Once, there was a canal.

But you aren't imagining yet
our shanty town lives.
Picture me as hired help,
cook and domestic servant,
the only female in a male barracks.
Or perhaps, if we are lucky, we board
in a house shared with other families.

Either way, I am not dressed in finery,
carrying a parasol, and waving a fan
when Daniel and I meet.
The camps are muddy and poor
and my clothes sweaty and worn,
my cheeks flushed from the soup kettle,
the cooking fire, the floor scrubbing,
my hair dull and unwashed.

I am only sixteen years old
and newly away from Mother and Father.
Every evening there is some bawdy
drunk flirting with me,
and other men fighting, swearing,
laughing, telling stories, singing,
teasing, protecting me like a sister,
vying for attention.

I am on guard against lewd advances,
lonely, fascinated, unsure, harried,
amidst so many unmarried men,
all aching for wives.

I am told daily
by the married women,
happy or disappointed with their husbands,
that I hold the reins.
There are dozens of possible suitors.
I can bide my time, wait
for an exceptional man.

How Daniel Courted Kate, 1843

Kate has no patience
for laziness or uncouth behavior,
and will surely spurn me too,
but here I am, this Sunday morn,
with a wildflower bouquet,
asking to walk her to church.

I am twenty-eight, far from family,
and, after six years in America,
more lonely than free.

I've never courted before.
In Indiana, life's been hard and poor.
But I need more than canal work and whiskey
and I've finally saved enough
to dream of farming good land
with strong, smart Kate as my wife.

I've watched the other fellows.
They all know life will be richer
with a woman like Kate.

Today she carries a bouquet
and walks beside me, glad
for a warm morning without work.

I've come to show her
what all the others
have failed to prove.

That her life will be richer
with a man like me.

Catherine Meehan Heffernan Described in a Few Words

Kate – we, your descendants,
must conjure you from
the few words that pepper
the biography of Daniel written
by your grand-daughter
who described you

as a woman, capable of fury,
who, when needed,
responded immediately,
raised cane all night,
and took matters in hand.

She says you asked your children
to read to you as you worked
and that you advised them to walk
barefoot to church to keep their shoes clean.

She says you were intelligent and practical,
a great influence, and frugal
manager of time and money.

She says the family came to you
to weigh every problem or need,
trusting you would pass judgment fairly
and, when you deemed a petition worthy,
you funded it from the flour barrel
where you kept spare gold.

Kate's Story While Shopping at Purdue, Brown, and Co.

When my pantry's empty, I come here
for salt cured pork, smoked ham, bacon,
lard, corn meal, wheat, flour,
sugar, cider, tea, pickles, and molasses.

Here, many times, I touched with longing
printed long or square shawls,
Irish linen, mulls, laces, edgings, inserts,
towels, napkins, silk cravats,
silk and cotton threads, silk hosiery.

I've tried on ladies gloves and winter mitts,
pictured Daniel in tailored shirts, jeans, linseys,
imagined all the things I could make
from brown and bleached sheetings and shirtings,
cotton and wool flannels, poplin, gingham, apron checks,
cotton, cashmere and alpaca yarn,
cotton warp, batting, wicking, buttons,
pins, needles, hooks, eyes, spun cotton,
cotton and patent pound thread.

This store makes me long
for a large family
and house of my own
in need of combs, brushes, brooms,
bedticks, rugs, floor mats,
and domestic carpeting
though I content myself
with the least expensive fabric to sew
work shirts and dresses from,
flour to make our bread.

Once, there was a canal.

Today, I've come for hairpins and diapers
and once again, Mr. John Purdue,
a man quite skilled at bargaining,
begs to adopt my blond-curled,
blue-eyed Michael, toddling at my side.

I emphatically tell
the prosperous merchant
if he offered me
all the fine things in the world,
I'd still say no!

Daniel at the Canal Dock

Sometimes I pause here
watching warehouse men
unloading and loading
the slow moving, mule-drawn
freight boats with names like
Odd Fellow, Queen of the Forest,
 and Green Eyed Kathy,
that arrive and depart
for cities far from here,
one after another,

and I imagine how someday
among these millions
of bushels and barrels
and crates of flour, salt,
barley, rye,
sugar, molasses,
coffee, tobacco,

stone, shingles,
nails, hoes, pitchforks,
mill stones,
beeswax, wool,
ash, lime

cheese, butter,
bacon, lard,
beef and tallow,
chickens, hogs,
beer, and whiskey,

will be the corn, oats,
and wheat grown
on land I've farmed.

Once, there was a canal.

Our History Keepers

The bards of old trained to be
the people's memory,
to stand on the breast of a hill
and hear the voices of long-dead warriors,
the wisdom of every root and branch,
the footfalls of those now dead
coming and going through the forests,
until after years of study each
pebble and leaf of changing landscape
contained an ancestral story they could tell.

Such history keepers are still among us.
They do not wear cloaks of woad or carry poet staffs.
They wear khakis and carry cell phones.
They share books, write books, write grants,
direct museums, study genealogy, paint murals.

They are women like Marge Graham, Carolyn Schmidt,
men like Bob Schmidt, Dan McCain, Terry Lacy,
and Tom Castaldi,
who will spend his day driving with you
from Delphi to Logansport,
pointing to the left, the right on Towpath Road,
saying, "Over there, on that hill
is a cemetery with canal builder graves,
and here is where the old tavern was,
and here is where the men drowned
when the bank gave way,
and here a lock, a bridge, a culvert was."

Part Three - From Summit City to Star City

When you stop for lunch he will admit
to having studied something about the canal
every day of his adult life,
shrugging his shoulders, saying,
"If it had been the Bible instead,
I'd be like a revival preacher by now,
able to quote the whole thing by heart."

Once, there was a canal.

PART FOUR

OUR MISFORTUNE RATHER THAN FAULT

I sat down to write about pain, and wrote, instead, about healing, history, and survival. The work revealed to me that there is a geography of the human spirit, common to all peoples.

   -- Linda Hogan

Part Four - Our Misfortune Rather than Fault

How Others Described the Irish

1. James Silk Buckingham, English Visitor, After Seeing
   a Work Camp on the Illinois and Michigan Canal

I never saw anything approaching
the scene before us, in dirtiness and disorder...
whisky (sic) and tobacco seemed
the chief delights of the men;
and of the women and children,
no language could give an adequate idea
of their filthy condition, in garments and person.
They are not merely ignorant and poor –
which might be their misfortune rather than their fault –
but they are drunken, dirty, indolent, and riotous,
so as to be the objects of dislike and fear
to all in whose neighborhood
they congregate in large numbers.

2. Charles Dickens, Touring a Shanty Settlement for Railroad Workers,
   Lebanon, Pennsylvania, early 1840's

With means at hand of building decent cabins,
it was wonderful to see how clumsy,
rough, and wretched, its hovels were.
The best were poor protection from the weather;
the worst let in wind and rain through wide breeches
in the roofs of sodden grass, and in the walls of mud;
some had neither door nor window;
some had nearly fallen down, and were
imperfectly propped up by stakes and poles;
all were ruinous and filthy.

Hideously ugly old women
and very buxom young ones,
pigs, dogs, men, children, babies,
pots, kettles, dunghills,
vile refuse, rank straw, and standing water,
all wallowing together in an inseparable heap,
composed the furniture of every dark, dirty hut.

3. James Mactaggart, Rideau Canal Official, After Viewing
Canal Workers Living in Caves Along the Ottawa River

Families contrive to pig together
worse even than in Ireland.
You cannot get the low Irish
to wash their faces,
even were you to lay before them
ewers of crystal water and scented soap;
you cannot get them to dress decently,
although you supply them with ready-made clothes.
They will smoke, drink, eat murphies, brawl, box,
and set the house on fire about their ears,
even though you had a sentinel standing over
with a fixed gun and bayonet to prevent them.

4. Ann Royall, After Stagecoach Travel Shared with Canal Workers

They were eternally getting in and out,
and suffocating you with the stench of drunkenness.
They are, for the most part, covered with mud,
where they have rolled when drunk,
and never think of buying
a little trunk, or light valisse,
to carry their clothes from place to place,
but always have a wad of something tied up
in a black greasy old pocket handkerchief,
and crowd you, and grease you,
and stench you to death.

The Great Hunger – An Gorta Mór

Now everything that dreams dreams of hunger.
Even the frozen earth is ravenous,
swallows one after another lifeless body,
wrapped in cardboard and newspapers,
into toothless shallow graves.

Wild with starvation,
not one blighted tuber left to choke down,
the Indian meal, Peel's brimstone,
gone from the stomachs of storehouses,
we scale wind-blown cliffs for seagull eggs,
we eat seaweed, and indigestible grass,
sneak off and suckle blood
from the neck of some stranger's cow,
claw loose earth with padded feet,
and with dog teeth
rip apart the cold corpses
and drag arms and heads of dead friends
whose weddings we once attended,
away from the other dogs, so we can feed.

In the morning, not a scrap of grain
or garbage left in the land,
we lie frozen on the snow,
half-naked in rags,
black hollow-bodied crows,
our night-long death caws
now silent,

the nightmare worse
for those who wake
to starve another day.

Part Four - Our Misfortune Rather than Fault

Letter from Tipperary, Winter 1846

Dear Daniel and Kate –
Your happy news reached us here and gives us joy. It is an honor that you named your first child after Father and me. I hope this letter reaches you all – Daniel, Katie, and new little Michael – in good health and prosperity.

I must in turn share sad news with you. I have come to Father Healy to help me write this letter, as he does every day to help parishioners tell families in America the awful state of Ireland as our troubles continue.

I do not want to darken your spirits with this news, but must, so here it is. Earlier this month, mother was taken quite suddenly by the fever. We are all so thin you won't recognize us. Father misses mother sorely, his spirits weaker every day. I am glad you do not have to see him so defeated.

I and your brother John do what we can to find food for us all, but we can barely find the money for rent, which has gone up and up since you left in '37. What extra money I earn goes to purchase the Indian corn offered by the relief office. This meal is hard to stomach, but it and cabbage is near all we have had. I've taken some work on the roads. 'Tis hard labor but many are turned away so I am lucky to have it. I need the work to buy the corn.

I have never seen such despair. There isn't a man around who hasn't armed himself. In Clonmel, where shops brim with breads and cakes, and drays loaded with all of Tipperary's grain are brought to the wharfs, headed for England, there have been riots. If we weren't starving, and had more strength, many more men would take to such extremes.

I hoped the potatoes planted this spring would be free of last year's blight. These hopes were blighted themselves last month, when again on our few acres, and all the other plots around us, the stench and rot set in, not sparing a single tuber. I knelt in the field, glad pouring rain hid my tears.

Once, there was a canal.

Father Healy urges me to tell how every day a letter arrives in the parish mail
from America, the post office full of them, and many with money in them
from some family member sending what help they can to those they love
struggling and starving in Ireland, nothing for us here but poverty and distress.

I must remind you of the promise given before you left, when Anne needed
a dowry and I gave my passage money to her with your assurance you would
send money for me to join you. I have not asked for it while your letters
described hardships and trials and often complained of how the scrip
you are paid is sometimes nearly worthless. But in your recent letter
you convey more optimism. Given our hunger and increasing fear
of violence, I hope you may now have the means to honor your promise.

I find strength in imagining that next year I will see your bridge over
the Wabash, and kiss the cheek of my namesake nephew. We have seen
horrors here I will not speak of. Ireland has become a nightmare.

Your loving brother, Michael Heffernan

Newly Married Kate Takes Matters in Her Own Hands, 1847

Yes, I read the letter as soon as it arrived
and I was infuriated and frightened.

It took weeks for it to travel by ship and canal.
It will take weeks for our response to reach Tipperary.
What if it was already too late to help?

I wrote back, hands shaking, not waiting for Daniel.
I took from the flour bin all the money
we could spare and sent it to Michael.

We fought, Daniel and I, as we had never done,
him saying, "Kate, Kate! that money
was for the land, the life I promised you.
Now there isn't enough and instead of finally
settling, I'm forced to keep working the canals!"

And me saying, "How could you
not have told me of your promise to him?
And how could you have lived with yourself,
not keeping it? And how, could we
ever be happy, starting our life together,

or be at peace with, worthy of,
the life that money might have bought,
knowing we are ignoring such
horrible suffering back home?"

Michael Heffernan Fills in Some Missing Details, 1848

I wanted to use all Dan's money
to buy food for those still living
but they would not let me.
Still I left them as much of it
as I could before saying goodbye.

The ship from Cork was crowded,
near three hundred squeezed below
in makeshift decks where timber was loaded
before and after us. We were given bread,
and rice to cook, though then
our ration of water was not enough
to quench our thirst.

We cooked and shat and slept
each in our few feet of space,
and the hold smelled like a cesspool.
Then fever began to spread,
a little girl playing one day
would be screaming for water the next;
an orphaned boy, huddled forlornly
in his dead father's coat; canvas-covered
corpses lining the hold and on we sailed
praying and dreaming beside them.

When we finally reached the St. Lawrence,
half the passengers were dead or sick with typhus,
with more than forty boats ahead waiting
their turn to disembark at Grosse Isle.
By the time I came ashore, thousands
lay sick, in their own filth, and a thousand more
were dead, the priests and gravediggers
unable to keep up with burials.

I made it out and traveled on
through towns where fever spread
as we arrived, too soon out of quarantine,
homeless, or seeking an address
carried in pocket or cardboard suitcase,
guarded, memorized, more precious
than passport or gold.

I boarded a steamer and sailed to Toledo,
then rode the canal, drifting slowly through Indiana,
the meals of pork, pickles, and cider,
the canvas cot suspended from the packet's ceiling,
all welcome luxuries compared to what I'd survived
to reach the wharf at Lafayette and enter
your grandmother's story as a "funny little man,
who strolled down the middle of the street,
talking to everyone, dressed in an old straw hat
with the top out, a fine mop of hair sticking

out the top, and inquiring, with a shy grin,
when my sister-in-law opened the door,
'Would you be Katie?'" leaving all the rest
of this story, behind me, untold until now.

Kate's Middle of the Night Confession

Again we are leaving.

But now I go as mother instead of child,

a mother with a three year old son,
and baby Ellen at my breast, to keep safe,

a mother worrying that I will lose them,
that this choice to leave
will lead us to the place
where they will be taken
too soon from my story
before living their own.

Again, I've woken
in the middle of the night,
remembering my baby sister,
my three-year old brother,
and my mother's unending grief
when they were lost to her,
erased from our lives,
before we reached America.

We will leave in the morning,
Daniel and I and our young ones,
Uncle Mike, as we call him,
still gaunt but gaining
and eager to work,
and my brother John,
his Mary and baby Mary.

We will travel south,
through more cholera
toward promise
of a bridge being planned
over east White River.

Part Four - Our Misfortune Rather than Fault

We have each other,
a family traveling together,
to counter the feeling
of belonging nowhere.

And still, there will be times,
like now, I lie awake in the dark,
adrift between the unredeemable
past and the unknown future,
feeling how as a mother
my whole body is
woven through, bound to,
the well-being of others.
Unable to protect them enough,
I am afraid to feel –
and have to feel –
how much I need and love them.

My life goes with them
whatever happens,
life or death,
and if I lose them,
nothing will remain inside me
but some scrap,
the child I was,
but without her mother,
left to handle
the rest of life
alone.

Cholera, August 1849

We, the physicians of Lafayette and Rev. Wilson and Father Clark, the only
clergymen who have not fled, do not know what causes this intestinal
affliction. It may be carried in the atmosphere by a miasma emanating
from putrescent matter, atmospheric influences, the malarial of decaying
vegetation, unripe and unwholesome provisions, impure water, imperfect
ventilation, and it may be that those who are susceptible to this poisonous
atmosphere have weakened themselves by leading an immoral or intemperate life.

We advise you to keep a digestible diet, exclude alcohol and all vegetables
except boiled potatoes, wear flannels to protect from cold and damp, avoid
the influence of grief, fear, anxiety, and stay calm because terror is apt
to excite this malady. Seek a doctor's help for any derangement of stomach
or bowels. Beware of various patent medicines and cholera nostrums
gotten up by quacks, panaceas not fit for slop sinks.

Now constantly on the go, night and day, visiting the sick, burying the dead
(47 this week), we implore the Almighty to stay the destroying hand now
lifted up against us, and urge all townsfolk to continue their ordinary duties,
engage in reciprocal interests with those around us, act to relieve the afflicted –
succoring the sick, burying the dead, looking after the needs of survivors.

And we pray that this suffering serves to constrain our attention to evils
long neglected, so that our city, great emporium of trade on the upper Wabash,
bustling county seat, home to more than six thousand residents, is blessed
amidst this misfortune by all possible effort toward the cleaning of our streets
of the effluvia of very crowded residences and the accumulation of filth to which
the lazy, ignorant and foreign born are prone, drying up the fountains of disease,
establishing sanitary regulations, promoting habits of frugality and temperance.

Part Four - Our Misfortune Rather than Fault

Once, there was a canal.

PART FIVE

IN PIKE AND DAVIESS COUNTY

And following its path, we took no care
To rest, but climbed: he first, then I-- so far,
Through a round aperture I saw appear
Some of the beautiful things that Heaven bears,
Where we came forth, and once more saw the stars.

   --Dante Alighieri

This acknowledgement of my ancestors provided ballast for my life;
it restored a foundation that had been missing, one from which I could
move more deeply into relationship with the wider world. This is a form
of ancestral soul retrieval each of us can do. As we do so, we become
better able to set our souls into this soil and become indigenous on this land.

   --Francis Weller

Part Five - In Pike and Daviess County

Once, there was a canal.

What Daniel Read and Responded To

Notice To Contractors – Terre Haute, April 23, 1849

Canal Letting.

The Trustees of the Wabash and Erie Canal,
hereby give notice that they
will receive sealed proposals
at Washington, Davies (sic) county, Indiana,
on the 27th day of June next,
for the construction of about
twenty-four miles of said Canal,
extending from the proposed Dam
across the West fork of White River
near the South line of Green (sic) county,
to Maysville, in Davies (sic) county.

On this portion of line
are to be constructed
five Lift Locks and one Guard Lock,
to be built of timber,
a Dam across Slinkard's Creek,
and one or two small Aqueducts,
together with the usual
variety of earth work
common to a canal.
The line will be divided into sections
averaging about half a mile in length.

Part Five - In Pike and Daviess County

At the same time and place,
proposals will be received
for building, with cut stone masonry,
the piers of the Aqueduct
over the East fork of White River.
The stone for the masonry
must be procured from
the quarries of durable limestone
to be found on or near
either the East or West fork
of White River, from which point
they can be delivered by water.

The line to be placed under contract,
will be ready for inspection
ten days previous to the time of letting,
and all necessary information
in reference thereto will be
given by the Resident Engineer.

Daniel Describes His Work, 1851

The canal will never be finished.
As soon as a section is completed,
it must be repaired.
Embankments collapse.
Floods sweep away bridges,
stonework settles and shifts,
locks gates are washed away,
dams are vandalized.

It's a losing battle against nature,
a constant shortage of labor, money,
and men, all of us saying
if other work were as easily had,
we'd choose it without hesitation.

Work on the big bridges gives
some sense of accomplishment,
of building something with bones
that will outlast mine.

The covered bridge at Carrolton
was a great work, exciting
to be part of as a young man.
The longest bridge in Indiana,
a road and towing bridge –
I am proud I worked on it.

Part Five - In Pike and Daviess County

Then there was the toll bridge
over the river and canal
at Brown Street in Lafayette,
funded by merchants like John Purdue
a gregarious, bulldog of a man!
Surely he was joking about
wanting to adopt our little Michael.
'Tis true when we left Lafayette,
life in the shanties was hard.
But what kind of life
could an unmarried man of business
give the child compared to the love
of his parents, no matter how poor?

And now we here we are in Petersburg,
all of us in our little clan
of Heffernans and Meehans.
Plenty of canal work,
John and Mike hard at it
and I, a bridge man again.

This, the longest aqueduct on the canal,
will be my last effort for this infuriating ditch,
which is why, as the sun sets,
I am carving my initials
into one of the bridge's beams.

Mr. A.J. Hart is hiring men to work
in Daviess County on the Ohio and Mississippi.
He says railroads are the future
and I have a job with him, if I want it,
and since we can't get clear title
to the land we tried to buy here,
I told him this morning I'll take it.

Once, there was a canal.

Letter from Kate to John Purdue, Summer 1852

Dear Sir, I am writing in hope
that you remember your acquaintance
with us, during the years 1843 – 48,
when we lived in Lafayette.

My husband, Daniel,
was foreman of the crew of men
who worked on the Brown Street bridge.
We were often in your dry goods store
with our small son, Michael.
You were so fond of him, you half-teased
you would adopt and spare him
the hard life of canal workers.

It seems that fate has caused
our lives to become entwined
with yours again.

After leaving Lafayette,
we travelled south to Petersburg,
where Daniel worked on the aqueduct
over the East Fork of White River.
We tried to purchase farmland there
but problems with a faulty title
made this purchase impossible.
We moved on to Montgomery in Daviess County,
where Daniel worked to lay tracks
for the Ohio and Mississippi railway line.

Part Five - In Pike and Daviess County

This spring, we recently purchased
eighty acres, where we have begun
to farm and build a homestead.
Here we hope to raise our, now, three children.

However, we have recently received news
that a suit has been brought against us
by an heir of the former owner of this land.
Apparently, your business ventures
connect you to the heir
and the suit to take this land from us.
Surely you do not know it is our family
such efforts will displace if successful.

I am writing to you to ask that,
as an old friend of ours,
you might help us
in any way possible.

Yours, sincerely,
Mrs. Daniel Heffernan

Once, there was a canal.

John Purdue's Response

Dear Mr. and Mrs. Heffernan,

I received your letter
and am writing to inform you
that I have withdrawn my interest
in the land to which you refer.

Had I known the suit was
was to be filed against old friends
I would not have become involved.

You should be informed
of a little known legal statute
stipulating that any heir to land here
must already reside here
at the time it is inherited.

When the case comes to trial,
if the heir testifies, under oath,
that she came to this country
after her father's death,
the suit should be
thrown out of court
on this technicality.

I am happy your family is well
and hope you have many years
of prosperous farming
to look forward to.

Sincerely,
John Purdue

Daniel, Summer Dusk on the Homestead

I've planted corn and oats for three summers now.
Every bushel harvested is balm to an ache
I'd forgotten was there the day I was born,
sowing itself into my dreams every night
I went to sleep, a hungry child.

I have chickens, cows, potatoes, and wild blackberries
to feed my family and two more baby girls
born here in the house I built.

Every evening I pause by the creek
and listen for the dove's call, the frogs,
the crickets, and I watch the moon
glide through slow clouds,
a packet boat drifting along.

I look for the fox at the far line of trees,
the setting sun sparking her eyes
as she turns and lopes across the field.

I know where her den is.

I know where the dove has built her nest.

I know where an acorn I planted
our first autumn here
is now a small seedling among old trees
on the far side of the creek.

I know the curved pattern
the plow makes through the earth,
the rise and fall of the land,
its hills and low swales.

Once, there was a canal.

I know each individual knot
in the pasture fence railing.

I know our animals,
the horses, the milk cows
by the sound of their breath,
their hoof-falls.

I know Orion's belt will lie in a line
over the roof of the barn all summer,
and, by winter, will have
turned sideways and become tangled
in the trees across the lane.

I can stand here and feel the world
slowly turning through the day,
tilting through the year.

I've walked this place into me.
I've worked this place into me.
I've breathed this place into me.

I've held fresh tilled earth in my palm.
Dew, sap, rain, mud, frost and deep snow,
the green stain of grass cut by my sickle
have seeped into my skin.

At first, I was so proud:
Everything here
belongs to me.

Now the feeling is
relief, gratitude, joy:
For the rest of my life,
here is where
I belong.

Nearing Sixty, Kate Speaks of Her Children

I gave birth to twelve – six boys, and six girls.
I've just buried another and pray that
the four sons, and three daughters left
will outlive me, comfort us in our old age.

Little Margaret was born not long after
we bought this farm. We'd built a small house,
two rooms and a loft, and hadn't yet added
the porch where we sit talking now.

She was our third girl in a row, and of course
Daniel had been hoping for another son.
But she just charmed us all, him most of all!
She had his bright blue eyes, you see,

and then, a few years later, we had Mary,
another girl! Poor Daniel said there must be
something in the water round here. He was
always kind enough to give me time, you know,

to get over one before we tried for another,
but this time I agreed to hurry myself along,
for Daniel's sake. So John came the next year

and Daniel was so proud! We named our first
after Daniel's father and brother, who joined us
from Ireland just after Michael was born. So now
we named our second son John, after my father

and my brother, who introduced me to Daniel.
But poor Johnny never got his strength,
and I wondered if, having him so soon after Mary,
maybe I was too depleted, and that affected him

Once, there was a canal.

even before he was born. He died near to
his first birthday and that broke our hearts.
I wanted to have another son, but couldn't bear
getting pregnant again while grief weighed me down.

But I knew Daniel was grieving too.
As soon as I felt myself rallying,
I prayed for God to bless us and two years,
almost to the day, after John's death,

William was born. He grew up such a bookworm,
and after adventuring west, prospecting for gold,
he came back to Daviess County and became a lawyer.
We are so proud of him for starting that Savings and Loan!

The year after Bill was born, though,
bright, blue-eyed Margaret caught a fever
that took her from us. She was only eight
and we were lost. To be honest, I was angry

with God for taking such a sweet, bright, curious girl
from us so soon! Then, a few months later,
I found I was pregnant again, with Thomas,
our eighth child. By then I was thirty-six

and feeling spent and I talked to Daniel
about this being our last. I said, "I've
been having babies since I was nineteen
and have done my duty as a good Catholic wife!"

But we went on to have four more!
I was forty-seven when I had James,
and just after I had told Daniel I was pregnant,
our oldest, Michael, told us to look forward to

Part Five - In Pike and Daviess County

our first grandchild! Born only weeks apart,
James was uncle to Biddie, who was his same age!
And Biddie came to live with us. A few days
after she was born, her mother died, bless her soul.

Of course, I took Biddie in and nursed her
as if I'd birthed them both, and she and James
grew up like twins. And now this, the hardest
loss I've ever faced, James' leaving us.

He was my last, my baby, and only twelve.
Daniel thinks it is his fault, but I don't
blame anyone, not even God this time.
Accidents happen on farms. There isn't

a family in a hundred miles around
who doesn't have a story about losing,
or nearly losing, a child from a fall,
a trampling, a fire, a drowning.

And poor Biddie's out of her head with grief.
She was there when it happened and the doctor
can't do anything to stop her tremors. Father Pierre's
come here nine days now, trying to chase away

her demons, by praying a novena for her
with us here at the farm, and at St. Peter's.
It's all he can do. It's all any of us can do.
Pray and wait for the heartache to fade.

When I Ask for More of Her Story

Great-great grandmother Kate Meehan Heffernan
comes to visit, just shows up one morning.
I take her to the farmer's market, library, supermarket.
We come home with potatoes and leeks grown in Daviess County,
an audio book of Mark Twain's Life on the Mississippi,
sushi, and honey in a plastic bear
because she is quite curious and laughs easily
about today's odd and unexpected things.

We chop potatoes and make potato-leek soup
and Irish soda bread, old favorites for both of us,
talking while we cook.

She asks a flurry of questions.
Baffled by how different my life is from hers,
she wants to know the history of these changes.

I say I wish I could visit her time, live there for a while,
the only way to know what her life was like,
and she ends up staying with me for a week, then another,
riding with me in the car, hanging out at my work,
sitting silently in the corner observing me do therapy,
crying sometimes from the stories we hear.

At first she is most comfortable
talking about what she likes
(the refrigerator, washer and dryer are favorites)
and doesn't like (the speed, the loneliness,
the disconnection from land and seasons horrify her).

She watches the news and the Daily Show with me,
mutters that politics now are as crazy as then.
We talk about immigration, gay marriage, marijuana,
the Middle East, her stance on abolition,
temperance, and women's suffrage.

When she learns I don't attend mass, she is distraught,

Part Five - In Pike and Daviess County

but listens as I explain how my parents,
like many after World War II, left the church.
When I tell her how I pray, and what I've learned
from Merton, Levertov, Teilhard de Chardin,
Hildegard of Bingen, Richard Rohr,
and the Sisters of Providence (whom she knew
as fellow pioneers, teachers of her children),
she softens and we watch Pope Francis on the internet
and read Mary Oliver and Wendell Berry poems together.

She begins to pour her heart out and listens
as I pour out mine. She tells me about loving
Daniel passionately though he infuriated her,
the many times she wished he would leave her
in peace so she wouldn't get pregnant again
and that, if she lived life over, she would birth
every one of her twelve children,
even knowing she'd bury five.

She refuses to hear me say, compared to her,
I have no right to complain of exhaustion
with only one child to raise. She insists,
"I had a whole brood of helpers. You don't,
and work hard, shoulder a heavy load.
Some things may be more easy,
but much is more cruel in your time."

Then suddenly, it is time for her to go.
She tells me how she missed her sisters
after moving to Montgomery with Daniel
and leaving now feels as painful as that.

I say I feel like she is the mother
I needed close by for so long
and she reassures me she will return.
"I can't stay forever," she says,
"but I can pop in and out, never far away.
Anything at all you need, just ask!"

Two-Thousand Grandmothers

Forty thousand years ago
an early human, possibly Neanderthal,
pressed her palm against
the rough, cool surface of a cave wall
and, using her hand as the first stencil,
blew through a hollow bone
a mouthful of paint
ground from iron oxide,
mixed with clay, spit,
animal fat, marrow and blood.

Through her, every twenty years or so, a new descendant.
Each new child touching the world with curious palms.
Two thousand generations later,
here are my hands, my fingers, my wrists,
resting on the surface of a laptop,
typing letters on the keyboard,
shaping words to bring to life
my great-great grandmother's story.

In a matriarchal chain,
only two thousand wombs between me
and that first artist.
Only two-thousand grandmothers.

Imagine how quickly,
how easily,
in our crowded world,
we could paint a subway wall
with two-thousand handprints.

What My Great-Great Grandparents Touched

Peat. Thatch. Potatoes pulled from the earth.
Newly sheared fleece. Irish rain. The milk cow's teats.

The work-warmed worn wood handles
of the butter churn, shovel, hammer, awl.

Wool as it is being spun, as it is being knit.
Cotton thread, an old silver thimble, a sharp needle.

Rosary beads. Some schoolbooks, chalk and slate.
The family Bible. Newspapers with stories of America.

The calloused, skilled hands of their mother and father.
Their own faces when tired, in thought, weeping.

The last embrace of those they said goodbye to.
A pebble palmed from the lane as they left home.

The wooden cradles of the ships that carried them.
Pots of dinged steel for urine and vomit tossed to the sea.

The first pebbles pocketed after coming ashore in New York.
The railing of steamships. Faded boarding house upholstery.

The shanty door latch, corn-husk pallets, ashes, whiskey flask.
A compass, ruler, pencils to draw bridges and aqueducts.

A rag doll. Leather shoes, beyond repair. Ribbons for braids.
Shell combs for a woman's bun. Hatpins and quilts.

Hands, lips, faces, each other's body on their wedding day.
Wages paid in Blue Dog and Red Dog scrip. Letters from Ireland.

Once, there was a canal.

Umbilical cords, placentas, amniotic fluid, blood from childbirth.
The same stuff as calves, lambs, and foals were born.

The axe and plow working an eighty acre farm. Seeds planted.
Weeds pulled. Harvests of corn, string beans, potatoes, milk, eggs.

Each newborn's hair, sunbeams, darkening, becoming human.
The family pew at St. Peter's. Grave markers for dead children.

Sarsaparilla root. Corn starch. Salt. Bread dough. Lard. Cast iron
skillets. Lye soap. Shaving cream on a brush. Talcum powder.

Newspapers with headlines about John Brown, Gettysburg,
Lincoln's death, Wounded Knee, the Wright brother's flight.

Shards of broken crockery. Buffalo nickels, Indian pennies.
Train tickets. Telegrams. Ballots. Bills of sale. Deeds.

Maps that showed Western territories becoming states.
McGuffey's Readers, loaned by nuns at the parish school.

Lilacs from the bush planted near the bedroom window.
Water from the hand-pump by the back door.

Gray hair brushed loose, given to the wind. Tears cried
on each child's wedding day. New-born grandbabies.

The tiny fingers of the infant who would become
my grandmother and hold me as baby.

The shawl of an old woman. The cane of an old man.
His hand in hers, holding on tenderly, as she lets go.

At Ninety-Two, Daniel Looks Back

Kate's been gone these five years now
and I haven't stopped missing her.
We were married fifty-seven years
and what she put up with, marrying me –
a stubborn canal man, too fond of whiskey,
and another bridge to build, a farm to work,
far from her mother, father, and sisters.

Now here it is, Easter Sunday, and spring is coming.
I've hobbled up the steps to sit in our pew at St. Peter's
and watch the sun fill the red, blue, and green glass
in our St. Patrick's window. Spring was Kate's
favorite season, and mine too, and every year
we always said it reminds us of Ireland –
the rain, the greening, the wind, the sea-gray clouds.

It's been seventy years since we both left there.
Seventy years! And like Kate, I will always miss it,
hard as life was, impossible as it was to stay.
Leaving was like dying, and making a life here took learning
to be in the world all over again. I hope, I believe,
Ireland would be proud, how I, one of her wandering sons,
have worked hard, and lived as I have lived –

not a great, but an honest, and a good life.
The canal is gone. All that work, so many men,
and years, and then abandoned not long after
it was finished. Not that it was every really finished.
Never fulfilled their grand dream, but nothing
a man makes ever does. It served its purpose –
got things and people moving, business booming.

Once, there was a canal.

Didn't surprise me when they shut it down.
It was a feat of engineering, a grueling challenge,
another crazy gamble, man against nature.
But it was honest work. My way of getting a toehold
in a world that would just as soon trample a poor man
as bid him welcome. My bridges stand, though no more
mules and packets, now trains and automobiles cross them.

I have sons to carry on the farm, and grandchildren
as strong and well-educated, and busy with commerce
as any of those Americans who, when I first arrived,
called the Irish low and the immigrants undesirable.
I brought the Heffernan clan safe ashore where
we will thrive. Today, I feel glad to be alive,
and hale enough to live another five years, even ten.

Though when I go, I will be glad to feel my spirit
flying over the farm, knowing it is part
of every tree, the stream, the corn, the earth,
and feel it turn and float toward the river,
the old bridge, and then west, and north,
up the noble Wabash, tracing all the remnants
of the old towpath, the canal bed, remembering

the work songs and rough voices of the navies,
and then lifting up, fast, over the Atlantic
back to Tipperary, again, at long last,
for one more visit, a slow stroll
down the familiar paths, up the lane
to the old cottage, slipping through our front door,
lingering by the peat fire before journeying on.

Communion

I've been told
it is possible
for the living
to return from visits
to the land of the dead
if, while there, we
do not eat or drink.
Not a sip. Not a morsel.

I began visiting the dead
cautiously, planning a brief visit —
a bit of genealogy,
a few old buildings,
a walk on the old towpath,
in and out, then on
with ordinary life.

But each tidbit offered
by the ancestors
invited me deeper in.

I forgot old warnings.

I found nourishment
I'd never tasted before
or imagined or knew
I was starved for.

I don't want to leave,
am glad our worlds overlap.

Once, there was a canal.

The ancestors need to feed us.
And we do not live until, fed by them,
we offer them feasts
of thanksgiving and longing.

When among the living,
I must place on my table
extra bread and milk
for the spirits
who surround and beckon.

And in their dark realm,
I will eagerly swallow
their ghost seeds,
which make me rooted.

Appendices

Once, there was a canal.

appendices

Appendices

Afterword: A Poet's Pilgrimage on the Wabash and Erie Canal

Embarking on a Writing Journey

I often write about relationships. To widen my exploration of this theme, I sought a project outside my autobiographical comfort zone. I turned to a brief family narrative describing the lives of my Irish immigrant great-great grandparents Daniel Heffernan and Catherine Meehan, who came to Indiana in the 1830's and worked to build the Wabash and Erie Canal.

As a child, I loved reading biographies of early Americans and yearned to be told stories of my family as pioneers. Yet the family story of Daniel and Kate did not come to my attention until I was an adult. Our hectic lives and families are so scattered that we have insufficient time for stories of great-great grandparents. We have forgotten to keep such stories alive.

For over 25 years, I have worked as art psychotherapist witnessing adults heal from traumas that have left them in pieces. Through this work, I became attuned to how fragmented and disconnected our world, our culture is. I understand that my feelings – of loss, grief, spiritual homelessness, isolation from community, and struggle to maintain a sense of belonging – are not symptoms of character flaws or individual wounds. Everyone I know feels these struggles. They are evidence of cultural trauma.

I began to hope that, if I came to know more fully the story of my great-great grandparents, I would find renewed connection to the world. I also hoped this project would rewake my childhood love of history. In the summer of 2015, with funding from the Indiana Arts Commission, I embarked on a journey to learn about the canal, wander small Indiana towns, walk remnants of the old towpath, meet with historians and genealogists, and visit museums and history centers. These travels offered a welcomed respite from explorations into painful, personal histories in the therapy room.

I love walking old paths that others traveled before me and soon realized that by following the canal's path, retracing steps of ancestors, I have undertaken a pilgrimage. Like all pilgrimages, my personal journey became connected to a larger communal journey, including Indiana's 2016 celebrations of its bicentennial.

Once I began, unexpected, synchronistic things started happening. A woman, whose great-great grandmother was my great-great grandmother's sister, emailed me out of the blue. This 4th cousin works in the Allen County Public Library's genealogy center. She was there, waiting to help me start my research the day I arrived in Fort Wayne. Time overlapped. History came alive. A modern Native American woman sat talking on her cell phone beside a tree on the treaty grounds where the Miami tribes gave up the land upon which the canal was built. My first full day of travel between Fort Wayne and Peru happened to be the one-day-per-year that the old steam engine, the Wabash Cannonball, comes to life, carrying passengers through the same towns. The tracks for trains like these were built on routes made earlier by the canal. I stood at a small town intersection near where the canal once flowed as the Cannonball thundered through and knew the thrill my ancestors must have felt for this monstrous beast. Just as they surely did, for the rest of that day, I found coal cinders on my skin and in my hair. That night I dreamed one of several dreams in which my ancestors visited me.

Research, Poetry, Fact, and Imagined Truth

With much to learn, I read thick books on 19th century Ireland and America, which, though they devoted mere pages to the canals, immersed me in the broad context of my ancestors' lives. I joined Ancestry.com to uncover additional family history. I joined the Canal Society of Indiana and studied their newsletters and canal history tour books. I learned about how canals are engineered and built. As a poet, I wasn't going to write in detail about canal engineering or the politics of Catholic Emancipation in Ireland. But I needed to know about these things to write poetry that brought to life the felt experience of Daniel and Kate. I learned that the word research means to search and search again. I went round in circles in my study of history, and my understanding grew each time I cycled through increasingly familiar terrain.

After months of searching, one poem about the potato famine or boat travel to America would finally piece together. Pages of studied material would condense into a single poetic line, mentioning one particular detail – a cardboard suitcase, a canvas cot - that precisely conveyed vast historical context through the eyes, hands, feet – the embodied perspectives – of my great-great grandparents.

But at this pace, I feared, I would run out of time and energy. The research felt burdensome; the writing too slow. I took boxes of books and notes with me for a weeklong winter retreat in a straw bale cabin by St. Joseph's lake at St. Mary of the Woods. I chose this spot because of its history. Here, Mother Theodore Guerin and the Sisters of Providence – who arrived in Indiana shortly after my ancestors – founded both a convent and college. In their teaching missions around southern Indiana, some of these first Sisters must have taught Daniel and Kate's children. In the cozy cabin, during the coldest week of the winter, in delicious solitude, I wrote. Some days, three poems would fly out first thing. Other days, the morning disappeared as I searched books and photocopies to clarify something I didn't understand. Often, late in the evening, unexpected poems bubbled up. I began to hear the voices of Daniel and Kate, and other ancestors as well. I had travelled deep enough into the project that they now had my full attention.

In the brief narrative I inherited, there are several threads for which I will never find actual historical documentation. For example, Daniel's sister Anne is mentioned but no record of her life after Daniel left Ireland remains. Also, Kate's story reveals that she came to America as a child with her mother, father, and many siblings. But no records other than baptismal dates in Ireland remain of her younger brother and baby sister.

As the ancestors began to speak, plausible stories answering my unanswerable questions emerged. In the poem in which Kate's mother, Ellen, describes travel from Ireland to Fort Wayne, she says that her two children died during the passage to America. Since no record remains of these children after the family reaches America, my choice to join a likely (but unverifiable) story with factual fragments helped me feel Ellen's grief for the loss of her children and thus enter into true and real feelings she would have known.

In fact, because bare genealogical dates of births and deaths lack an overall narrative or story, the circumstances of every death described in the poems had to be imagined. I found the poems worked best when I alluded to each death indirectly. Showing my ancestors' deaths through partial glimpses, I felt the grief of a mother who has lost a child, a husband outliving his wife of fifty-some years. My boldest fictional invention was to say a farming accident caused the death of Kate's youngest child, James. I do not provide specifics details of the imagined accident. But it seems likely that James died in a sudden way given the traumatic reaction to his loss of his niece Biddie (who was more like his twin sister).

My grandmother's narrative also mentions several letters written or received by Kate. None of these letters remain. So, I enjoyed recreating them. I read letters from Ireland sent during the Great Hunger and used their language and flavor to compose a fictional letter written by my great-great uncle, Daniel's brother, during the potato famine, as well as Kate's response sending passage money. I read a biography of John Purdue, Lafayette businessman and founder of Purdue University, in order to create a fictional letter from Kate to him, and his response.

Other fictional elements of the poems include decisions I made about what happened in Daniel and Kate's lives in between the few specific details I knew. For example, the family narrative states that, while living near Lafayette, Daniel worked to build "a bridge over the Wabash." I found two possible bridges, the Carrolton Crossing Bridge outside of Delphi, Indiana, and the toll bridge funded by John Purdue, at Brown Street in Lafayette. I decided that work on the Carrolton Bridge could have given Daniel experience that led him to work on the Brown Street Bridge. The dates of each bridge's completion lined up with events in my ancestor's lives, and Daniel's work on the Brown Street Bridge could explain how the Heffernan's came to know John Purdue well enough that, according to the family narrative, he asked to adopt their first child and later played a role in their buying land in Daviess County.

Through allowing fictionalized details to link with the narrative I'd inherited, the story grew more whole. Imagining what was lost was like rebuilding the long ago abandoned remnants of the canal so that I could finally navigate the entire arc of my great-great grandparent's lives.

Accepting the Food of the Ancestors

In addition to writing in my ancestor's voices, two other types of poetry emerged. I enjoy discovering the words of the past in actual letters and documents. To share some of these historic voices, I created "found" poems from these records. Actual statements of people from the canal era show how they thought about the canals, debated about the need to build them, advertised to find canal workers, and perceived the Irish immigrants who took that work. I include the sources for these poems at the end of the book.

I also wrote from a mythic perspective about following ancestral paths. I connected my writing to the old Celtic immram tales, stories of heroic voyages. I saw my great-great grandparents journeys to American and through Indiana as 19th century immrams that were as courageous and worth remembering as the tales of Celtic heroes, such as Bran, St. Brendan, Ossian who journeyed to Tír na nÓg on the horse of Niamh, as well as the goddess Brighid, muse of the bards. These mythic figures, with which my ancestors were familiar, entered my writing. As this mythic dimension deepened, I realized that my journey to reconnect with ancestors is akin to the journey that other poets, such as Virgil, Dante, Orpheus, are said to have taken to the land of the dead. I was participating in an essential practice of the ancient bards: keeping alive and telling the stories of our ancestors.

Before my winter's retreat, I commented to a friend that writing about ancestors is a form of grief-work. She reminded me of myths that say visitors to the land of the dead can return to their normal lives if they refrain from eating while in Hades. I responded immediately, "Then I will never fully return, because I am being deeply nourished by this work!"

At last, I understood what I had begun this project searching for. Through reconnecting with my ancestors, I had been doing what therapist and leader of grief rituals Francis Weller describes as "ancestral soul retrieval," a work that provides me with "ballast for my life" and restores "a foundation that had been missing" from which I can "move more deeply into relationship with the wider world."

I see this deepened relationship with the world in how I now smile at road construction crews whose bridge building, lane widening, and repairs make my daily commute longer and more frustrating. These men are doing work to make human travel possible that began before the Roman roads, was taken up by my great-great grandfather in early Indiana, and continues worldwide to this day.

I experience this deepened relationship with the world as I remember how the Irish were treated, and the opportunities that they still managed to find, as I listen to the news of politicians who want to build walls to keep people from crossing our borders and who debate about whether to allow Muslims into our country.

I feel this deepened relationship to the world when I stand in my own suburban yard, connected to Indiana in a more rooted way, because I have walked in places where my ancestors walked; I've touched the old limestone abutment of a bridge my great-great grandfather helped build; I've visited the old church where the 1890 window of St. Patrick, donated by Daniel and Catherine, bears their names; and I've stood on the soil that they once farmed, watching a combine harvesting this summer's corn.

Daniel and Kate spent much of their lives leaving behind a home that could not support them and finding their new home in America. I have spent much of my life feeling displaced and disconnected by constant change and the severing of communities (human and wild) that occurs in pursuit of "progress" and "development." Our cultural fear and avoidance of the past, of death, of remembering what was, insists that connection with such things will make us afraid, depressed, lost. Having dug a canal of poetry on which my ancestors and I now travel between our worlds, I find quite the opposite to be true. Connection with their past makes me stronger, more wholly rooted, and at home in ways I never knew before.

Appendices

Notes

Part One: Surveying The quotes are from: Herman Melville, Moby Dick. Black and White Classics: NY, 2012; Walt Whitman, "Song of Myself," Leaves of Grass. The First (1855) Edition: Brooklyn, NY, 2012.

The Path of the Earliest Surveyor, 1765 This poem quotes directly from the travel journals of early explorers to the area, especially the 1765 journal of George Crogahn, and the 1827 surveyor's log of John Peter Paul as cited in Thomas E. Castaldi's Wabash and Erie Canal Notebook – II, p. 1- 2.

From A Letter to His Excellency George Washington This poem quotes directly from Robert Fulton's letter to George Washington as included in The Hoosier Packet: News and Journal of the Canal Society of Indiana, Vol. 14, No. 8, Aug. 2015.

What the Governors Said – Hendricks, Ray, Noble, 1822-34 This poem quotes directly from the speeches of the early governors of Indiana, as found in Indiana House Journal, 1822-23, p. 38; Indiana House Journal, 1826-27, p. 42-44, and Indiana House Journal, 1834-35, p. 14, as cited in Indiana: From Frontier to Industrial Commonwealth, Volume 1. John D. Barnhart, Ph.D and Donald F. Carmony, Ph.D. Lewis Historical Publishing Company, Inc. New York. 1954.

Upon News of the Passage of the General Internal Improvement Bill – 1836 This poem quotes directly from both Paul Fatout's descriptions of statewide celebrations in response to this bill in his book Indiana Canals, Purdue University Press: West Lafayette, IN, 1972, p. 74 and also from the newspaper article, "A Report from Peru" in the Indiana Journal (Indianapolis), January 19, 1836 as cited in Barnhart and Carmony.

Part Two: Voyages on the Ancestral Path The quotes are from: John O'Donohue, "A New Year Blessing," in Benedictus: A Book of Blessings, Transworld Publishers, London, 2007; Wendell Berry, "The Real Work" in Standing By Words, Counterpoint: Berkeley, CA, 1983.

Part Three: From Summit City to Star City The quotes are from: Mark Twain, Life on the Mississippi, Dover Publications: Boston, 2000; Robert MacFarlane, The Old Ways: A Journey on Foot, Penguin Books: NY, 2012.

Appendices

Packet Boat Travel: Two Perspectives This poem quotes directly from packet boat travellers' written letters and descriptions of their travels, as found in Paul Fatout, Indiana Canals, Purdue University Press: West Lafayette, 1972, p. 135-139 and The Hoosier Packet: News and Journal of the Canal Society of Indiana, Vol. 11, No. 11, Nov. 2012.

Kate's Story While Shopping at Purdue, Brown, and Co. The list of materials in this poem is quoted directly form Robert Kriebel, The Midas of the Wabash: A Biography of John Purdue, Purdue Univ. Press: West Lafayette, 2002. p 31-33.

Part Four: Their Misfortune Rather Than Their Fault The quote is from Linda Hogan, "Geography: An Introduction" in The Woman Who Watches Over the World, W.W. Norton: NY, 2001.

How Others Described the Irish This poem quotes directly from the following sources: J. S. Buckingham, The Eastern and Western States of America, London, n.d, v. 3, p. 223-24; Charles Dickens, American Notes, and Reprinted Pieces, orig. ed. 1842, London, 1870, ch.10, p. 126; John Mactaggart, Three Years in Canada: An Account of the Actual State of the Country in 1826-28, London, 1829, v. 3, 243-44; Ann Royall, Mrs. Royall's Pennsylvania, or Travels Continued in the United States, Washington, 1829, v. 1, p. 126 all cited in Peter Way, Common Labour: Workers and the Digging of North American Canals, 1780-   1860, New York: Cambridge University Press, 1993, p. 144, 165-6.

Cholera, August 1840 This poem quotes directly from historical documents provided in J. Marshall, "Cholera in an Indiana Market Town: "Boosters" and Public Health Policy in Lafayette, 1849," Indiana Magazine of History, Vol. 98, Issue 3, 2002, p 169-202, from http://scholarworks.iu.edu/journals/index.php/imh/article/view/11928/17563.

Part Five: In Pike and Daviess County The quotes are from the Robert Pinsky translation of Dante Alighieri's The Inferno, Canto XXXIV, Farrar, Straus, and Giroux, NY, 1994, p. 303; Francis Weller, The Wild Edge of Sorrow: Rituals of Renewal and the Sacred Work of Grief, North Atlantic Books: Berkeley, CA, 2015

What Daniel Read and Responded To This poem quotes directly from a notice to contractors printed in the Canal Society of Indiana Tourbook, "The Final Link." Gibson, Pike, Daviess, Greene Counties, March 27-29, 1998, p. 55.

Canal Era Bibliography and Resources

Barnhart, John D. and Carmony, Donald F. Indiana : From Frontier to Industrial Commonwealth, Volume 1. Lewis Historical Publishing Company, Inc. New York. 1954.

Black, Harry G. The Miami, Wabash, and Erie Canal Country: An American Heritage. HMB Publications: Hammond, IN, 1991.

Canal Society of Indiana. Tourbooks "Along the Heritage Trail," "Crossing Waters," "Celebrating Canal Communities," "Across the Cross Cut," and "The Final Link".

Canal Society of Indiana. The Hoosier Packet. Monthly newsletter. Membership in society available through www.indcanal.org

Castaldi, Thomas. Wabash and Erie Canal: Notebook 1, Allen and Huntington Counties. Canal Society of Indiana: Fort Wayne, 2002.

Castaldi, Thomas. Wabash and Erie Canal: Notebook 2, Cass, Carroll and Tippecanoe Counties. Canal Society of Indiana, Fort Wayne, 1998.

Castaldi, Thomas. Wabash and Erie Canal: Notebook 3, Wabash and Miami Counties. Canal Society of Indiana: Fort Wayne, 2004.

Fatout, Paul. Indiana Canals. Purdue University Press: West Lafayette, IN, 1972.

Howe, Daniel Walker. What Hath God Wrought: The Transformation of America, 1815-1848. Oxford University Press, 2007.

Jenkins, Brian. Era of Emancipation: British Government of Ireland, 1812- 1830. McGill-Queen's University Press: Montreal, 1988.

Kelly, John. The Graves Are Walking: The Great Famine and the Saga of the Irish People. Henry Holt and Company: New York, 2012.

Kriebel, Robert. The Midas of the Wabash: A Biography of John Purdue. Purdue University Press: West Lafayette, IN, 2002.

Marshall, J. "Cholera in an Indiana Market Town: "Boosters" and Public Health Policy in Lafayette, 1849." Indiana Magazine of History, Vol. 98, Issue 3, 2002, p 169-202. http://scholarworks.iu.edu/journals/index.php/imh/article/view/11928/17563

Appendices

Poinsatte, Charles. Fort Wayne During the Canal Era, 1828-1855. Indiana Historical Bureau, 1969.

Reynolds, David S. Waking Giant: American in the Age of Jackson. HarperCollins: NY, 2008.

Way, Peter. Common Labour: Workers and the Digging of North American Canals, 1780- 1860. Cambridge University Press, 1993.

Once, there was a canal.

Wabash and Erie Canal: 1832 – 1876

Canal Timeline:

1827:   federal government land grant made to state of Indiana for what was to become the Wabash and Erie Canal

1832:   ground broken during ceremony in Fort Wayne, IN

1843:   canal opened from Lafayette, IN to Toledo, OH and Lake Erie, providing commercial access to eastern seaboard

1853:   canal completed to Evansville, IN on the Ohio River; from Toledo to Evansville, the canal's total length was 468 miles (second longest canal in the world)

1874:   canal abandoned by the State after decline accelerated by railroad improvements

1876:   canal right-of-way sold

Appendices

Map designed by Terry Lacy
Courtesy Wabash and Erie Canal Interpretive Center, Delphi, IN

About the Author

Poet Liza Hyatt is the author of The Mother Poems (Chatter House Press, 2014), Under My Skin, (WordTech Editions, 2012), Seasons of the Star Planted Garden (Stonework Press, 1999), Stories Made of World (Finishing Line Press, 2013), and Art of the Earth: Ancient Art for a Green Future (Authorhouse, 2007) an art-based eco-psychology workbook. Liza is an art therapist (ATR-BC, LMHC) who facilitates classes, workshops, readings, retreats, and therapeutic programs for numerous Indiana organizations. For more information, visit www.lizahyatt.com.

Appendices

Previous Publications

"What My Great Great Grandparents Touched" – on Indiana Humanities Council website's National Poetry Month daily Poem-and-Prompt feature, curated by Indiana Poet Shari Wagner, April 23, 2017. http://indianahumanities.org/great-great-grandparents-touched

"The Path of an Early Explorer, 1765" (then titled "Portage at the Carrying Place") – on Indiana Humanities Council website Poem-a-Day feature, curated by Indiana Poet Laureate George Kalamaras, April 2014.

"Immram Catherine Meehan" – Indy Writes Books edited by M. Travis DiNicola and Zachary Roth, Indianapolis, IN: Indy Reads Books, 2014.

"Two Thousand Grandmothers" – Reckless Writing 2013: The Continued Modernization of Poetry, Indianapolis, IN: Chatter House Press, 2013.

www.ingramcontent.com/pod-product-compliance
Lightning Source LLC
Chambersburg PA
CBHW080604170426
43196CB00017B/2900